The Naughty Bath Book for Grown-ups

Mike Cast

Cartoons by Roğ Bowles

HEADLINE

First published in 1994
by HEADLINE BOOK PUBLISHING

10 9 8 7 6 5 4 3 2 1

ISBN 0 7472 4809 5

Printed and bound in Great Britain by
The Bath Press, Avon

HEADLINE BOOK PUBLISHING
A division of Hodder Headline PLC
338 Euston Road
London NW1 3BH

CONTENTS

Acknowledgements 4

Introduction 6

The foreign tongue 8

Around the world in eight condoms 11

The history of the condom – so far 14

Star signs for lovers 17

Drinks to loosen up 19

Cock and Bull? 23

Why beer is better than women! 27

Why cucumbers are better than men! 30

Reasons for having sex in the bath 33

Tongue twisters and limericks 45

Bath-time sex games 48

The mother of all quizzes 52

Bath-time habits in the British Isles 56

Love is… 58

Coiffure of pubic hair 60

Weird sex 62

Dirty water guide 63

How much sex can I have? 64

What was that? 66

The history of soap 68

Soap operetta 70

Yes sir, no sir 72

Steamed up 74

A day in the life of Bartholomew (Barth for short) 84

Confessions of a plumber 86

Virgin on the ridiculous 89

Agony pages 92

Final thought for today 96

Acknowledgements

Calling all GRUBBIS (Grown-up's Bath Book Institute).

It started with *The Grown-up's First Bath Book* where, among many educational items, you could also learn to say 'My big toe is stuck in the tap' in Swahili. This led on to *The Grown-up's Bath Book of Puzzles and Fun*, which provided hours of fun including detailed instructions on things to make with your belly button fluff and now we have... *The Naughty Bath Book for Grown-ups*.

My co-author on this book is Roġ Bowles, who can only be described as utterly depraved and without morals, his able assistant Ron Cant (it's true), the vibrating Maxine and myself, a pillar of society. Our message to all our readers is 'GET F.I.T.T.' (Get Frolicking In The Tub).

Join us now and have some fun!

Mike Cast and Roġ Bowles

4

5

Introduction

In the Middle Ages, etiquette books decreed that hands, face and teeth must be washed frequently. Bathing was another story. King John of England was a shining example at variance with the general custom. He took a bath once every three weeks, and by so doing astonished his subjects with his fastidious ways.

The medieval method of bathing was a matey one. The entire family and their guests bathed together in a hand-filled round wooden tub, thus conserving hot water. Bath nights must have been merry occasions. Trays of food were set across the tub and musicians added to the gaiety of the scene. Other times – other customs. Medieval ideas of propriety differed vastly from those of today, despite the permissive society. No shyness then at being discovered ungarbed – knights, themselves armour-clad to the eyes, would sit companionably by in attendance upon ladies happily splashing in open-air baths. Not only did members of the opposite sex bathe together stark naked without hint of embarrassment, they all shared the one sleeping compartment as well, without night clothes. Such garments were never worn until the 16th century.

So why not slip back a few years and get stuck into the spirit of *The Naughty Bath Book for Grown-ups*.

The Foreign Tongue

There are more words in English than in any other language: more verbs, more nouns, more adjectives, more similes, more technical terms, more rhymes, more profanity and no doubt more swearing. So, while you are waiting for your partner to join you, how about having a go at the following less complex languages:

'That's not a loofah!'

GERMAN	Das is kein Luffaschwamm.
FRENCH	Ce n'est pas un luffa.
WELSH	Nid loofah yw hwn.
SPANISH	Esto no es un Estropajo.
MALAY	Jtu bukan loofah.
SWAHILI	Hilo Sio Dodoki.

'It's not clever and it's not funny... that's the loofah!'

'Sorry to dash your hopes, dear heart, but that's the loofah!'

10

Around the World in Eight Condoms

France
The French letter is referred to in French as 'le lettre anglais' – the English letter!

Lapland
A reindeer skin sheath.
'Bjorn pulled out his half thrall; her eyes opened wide with delight: "Give me a kiss… tonight will be bliss; it's the furry side outside tonight."'

China
They use the lower intestinal bile duct of the Tibetan yak. It sounds unlikely, but this is the same race that studied the excreta from the rear end of a worm and thought 'I'll spin that and make a nice suit'.

Malaysia
The instant latex line, produced from unnatural sex with a plantation rubber tree.

Australia

The 'aborigine's friend'. Similar to the didgeridoo made famous by Rolf Harris as a musical instrument, 'the didgeridon't'.

Africa

Aromatic leaves of the banyan bush. An optional extra for the Bantu with style, half a pineapple stuck on top.

Egypt

The baked dry condom. Triangular in section, of course, bound on with waxed papyrus string. Discovered among the personal effects of King Tutankhamun.

India

The meditation method, propounded by the Maharishi Rumpy Bumpy Yoyo, is a mantra chant: 'I will not co-o-o-me… I will not co-o-o-me.' As the booming population of India shows, the spirit is willing but the flesh is winning.

The History of the Condom – so far

100-200 AD Cave paintings at Combarelles, in the Dordogne, are said to show early use of the condom. One picture depicts a man and woman engaged in the act of coitus, with the man's penis seemingly covered.

1660s One of the favourite theories is that it was called after its inventor, Condom or Conton, or something similar, who was at the court of King Charles II.

Another theory is that it is derived from the Latin 'condus' which means receptacle.

1725–98 Casanova used condoms not only to prevent infection but to prevent impregnating his women friends. He referred to them by various names: 'Redingate Anglaise' (English Riding Coat), 'Lalottes d'assurances' (assurance caps). His only complaint was, 'I do not care to shut myself up in a piece of dead skin to prove that I am perfectly alive'.

1827 In Japan the condom was known as Kawagata or Kyotai, and was made of thin leather. Apart from this, the Japanese also used condoms made from tortoiseshell or horn.

1915 The foundations of the London Rubber Company were laid down in 1915 when L.A.Jackson set up as a 'wholesaler of chemists sundries' in one room behind a tobacconist's shop in the City of London.

In the early years condoms were imported, mainly from Germany, the major source in the 1920s.

1921 Marie Stopes and A.V.Roe opened the first clinic in the British Empire, for the distribution of contraceptive devices.

1939 When war broke out, German supplies of condoms were cut off and the London Rubber Company was left to try to satisfy a considerable demand, including orders from the armed forces. By rapidly expanding Durex condom capacity, output was tripled within a year and the wartime demand was met.

1957 First lubricated condom introduced.

1992 World's first-ever free-standing Durex vending machine installed at Nuneaton bus station.

1994 Competition launched in *The Naughty Bath Book for Grown-ups* to find out the most unusual uses for the condom in the bathroom – answers, please, using the inside of the old packet.

1995 In our next publication, *The Bath Book for Gardeners*, we consult an expert who looks at some of the uses for condoms in the garden!

Star Signs for Lovers

Pisceans do it on porpoise

Ariens do it with ramifications

Sagittarians do it with
their beaux

Geminians do it side
by side

Cancerians do it
sideways

Librans do it equally well

Taureans do it to udders

Scorpions do it with venom

Virgos do it immaculately

Leos do it with pride

Capricorns do it on inclination

Aquarians do it well

Drinks to Loosen Up

The Whip

1 part pastis
1 part dry vermouth
1 part brandy Curaçao

Shake, blend and pour into glass

First Night

2 parts brandy
1 part van der hum
1 part Tia Maria

Add tsp of cream, shake and then serve

Dirty Mary

1 part vodka
2 parts tomato juice
Angostura bitters

Shake and serve in a cocktail glass, Worcestershire sauce can be added

Tequila Steamrise

1 part tequila
4 parts orange juice

Pour over crushed ice in a tall glass. Add grenadine for sunrise effect

Parisian Blonde

1 part double cream
little caster sugar
1 part orange Curaçao
1 part dark rum

Shake well with ice, strain into cocktail glass. Decorate with orange slices

Fallen Angel

1 dash of Angostura bitters
2 dashes of green crème de menthe
juice of 1 lemon or half a lime
2 parts of gin

Shake well with ice, strain into cocktail glass

Did The Earth Move For You

1 part gin
1 part whisky
1 part Pernod

Shake well with ice, strain into cocktail glass

Between the Taps

1 dash of lemon juice
1 measure brandy
1 measure Cointreau
1 measure dark rum

Shake the ingredients well with ice and strain into a cocktail glass

'We were… er… I mean the wife was… er… reaching for the soap
when her head got stuck.'

21

Screw A Driver

1 part vodka
2 parts orange juice

*Pour over crushed ice, stir well,
decorate with orange slices*

Cock and Bull?

1 A woman from Surbiton drowned in her bath after a heavy love-making session.

2 A lady in Nuneaton was using a penis-shaped bar of soap to supplement her sexual activities which unfortunately broke off and now her husband boasts of the cleanest helmet in the world!

3 Pink Floyd is the technical name for a whale's penis.

4 The longest pubic hair is to be found on the Malarki tribe in the Amazon Basin who actually tie and plait their pubic hair!

5 Condoms used to be re-usable.

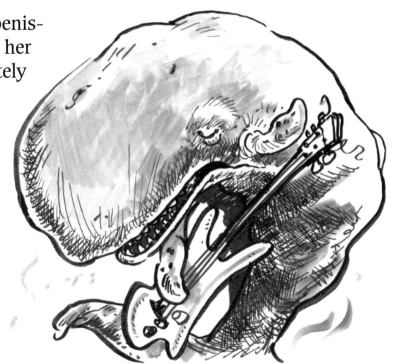

23

6 Seventy percent of British adults cannot spell erection.

7 After Nelson lost his arm at the battle of Santa Cruz he found great difficulty in washing properly, so he always took a bath with his trusted manservant.

8 More people wash the dog in the bath than have sex in the bath.

9 Cave paintings in the Dordogne are said to show early uses of the condom.

10 The longest recorded sex session in a bath lasted for over 62 hours in Atlanta, Georgia, with neither partner achieving a climax.

11 A London businessman caught his penis in a bath tap (cold) at the Hampton Court Hotel and had to be cut free by firemen.

12 The women of the African Bonkawayo tribe always give birth to their children in a mud bath.

13 Romans put peacock feathers down their throats at orgies to throw up and make room for more food and drink.

14 Caligula, the famous Roman emperor, made his trusted dog a consul.

15 Merkin is a word in the English dictionary and is a hairpiece for the pubic area (origin uncertain).

16 Prince Bandar bin Sultan bin Abdulaziz Al-Saud's home in Aspen, Colorado, has no fewer than 24 bathrooms.

17 The word Bartholomew comes from the New Testament and was the name of an apostle who spent a great deal of time bathing; the word can also mean to cleanse one's body.

18 Bath is an ancient Hebrew unit of liquid measure equal to approximately 8.3 imperial gallons.

Why Beer is Better Than Women!

You can enjoy a beer all month round

Beer stains wash out

You don't have to wine and dine beer

Your beer will always wait in the car while you play football, etc

When your beer goes flat, you throw it out

Beer is never late

A beer doesn't get jealous when you grab another beer

Hangovers go away

Beer labels come off without a fight

When you go to a bar you know you can always pick up a beer

Beer never gets a headache

Beer always goes down easy

A beer won't get upset if you come home and have another beer

You can have more than one beer in a night and not feel guilty

You can share a beer with your mates

You always know you're the first one to pop a beer

Beer is always wet

Beer doesn't demand equality

You can have a beer in public

A beer doesn't care when you come

A frigid beer is a good beer

You don't have to wash a beer before it tastes good

If you change beers you don't have to pay alimony

Beer doesn't sulk

Why Cucumbers are Better than Men!

The average cucumber is at least 6" long

Cucumbers stay hard for at least a week

You can fondle a cucumber in the supermarket and you know how firm it is before you get it home

A cucumber won't ask 'Am I the first?' or 'How was it?'

With cucumbers you don't have to be a virgin more than once

Cucumbers don't have sexual hang-ups

Cucumbers never need a round of applause

A cucumber won't make a scene if there are other cucumbers in the fridge

A cucumber will never give you a social disease

Cucumbers can stay up all night and you don't have to sleep on the wet patch

Cucumbers never leave you wondering for a month

Cucumbers won't compare you to a centrefold

It's easy to drop a cucumber

No matter how you slice it you can have your cucumber and eat it

Reasons for Having Sex in the Bath

'You'll definitely float!... bags I on top!'

1 You don't have a damp spot to avoid after.

2 Water is buoyant and far kinder than gravity... a saggy D cup will float magnificently.

3 You can make sure he's washed his willy.

4 You cannot wear spectacles in the bath... memory is far kinder than 20/20 vision.

5 Aliens find the sight of two humans mating excruciatingly funny... this is doubly so in the bath (quadruply so for aquatic aliens).

6 A bathroom door is easier to lock than a bedroom door... no fascinated enquiries from the younger part of the family.

7 Soapy water is a super lubricant – no friction burns or sore spots.

8 You can experiment with contraceptive techniques, ie. clench your hand rapidly in the water... see – a douche!

9 Water does not stay hot for ever... you have to set a time limit so you won't miss your favourite soap... on the box that is.

10 Pick soap that is the right shape and, with a little sleight of hand, you can be very impressive... 'Ooh that's big... hard, too.'

'If they're having so much fun, how come they're not laughing?'

35

'Don... the ceiling could do with another coat of emulsion.'

11 Anything with batteries in can be severely damaged... you can get back to some decent normal sex for a change.

12 Water supports bodies... you stand far less chance of having your nuts crushed.

13 Gone will be the sudden contact with cold feet to cool your ardour.

14 You don't have to scramble for tissues when your heart rate has returned to normal.

15 You can't play *Orca – Killer Whale* in a bed.

16 You won't feel so silly when he insists on wearing a snorkel!

17 Farting is much more fun than when under a duvet – you can make your own jacuzzi.

18 You can make the plumber's day when his friends start talking about someone having a mere toe stuck in the tap.

19 You can have as much fun with a water pistol as the kids.

20 Sex in the bath is like a well-known lager – it refreshes parts that you cannot normally reach.

'Whatever you've got in mind... forget it!'

'I draw the line at whinnying.'

'Wow! Whatever you just did, do it AGAIN!'

'Stop showing off!'

41

'T-I-G-E-R!! Guess what's hot and wet and waiting for you in the bathroo-oom!'

'WOW! The woman next door is hanging her clothes on the line and every time she stretches you can just see her knickers...'

43

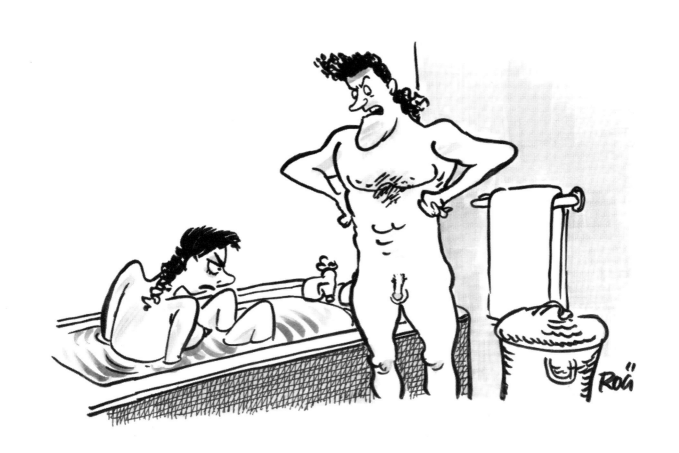

'WHO'S THAT GOING TO SATISFY?... ME of course!'

Tongue Twisters and Limericks

Is that a bare breasted booby bearing down on me?

Bertie Bubble bathed a batch of bimbo bathing beauties.

Penelope plopped her plimsolls in the plushy toilet pan.

Trevor towelled the trollop with a slimy chamois leather.

Picking partner's pubic hairs plastered in the plughole.

There was a young man from
   Caergwent
Whose tool was exceedingly bent.
One night to save trouble
He stuffed it in double
And instead of coming he went.

There was a young plumber from
    Lea
Who was plumbing his bird by
    the sea
Said the bird 'Stop your plumbing
There's somebody coming'
Said the plumber, still plumbing,
    'It's me!'

To his wife said the lynx-eyed
    detective
'Can it be that my eyesight is
    defective?
Has the east tit, the least bit
The best of the west tit
Or is it a trick of perspective?'

When your body's all covered in
    gunge
Attack it with loofah and sponge
For a vigorous scrub
When immersed in a tub
Ensures that the gunge you'll
    expunge

I think I should issue this warning
About taking a bath in the morning
You feel such a dope
If you swallow the soap
While laying there lazily yawning

A bath in a barrel for Perkin
Was all he desired after workin'
And after his scrub
He'd pop to the pub
For beer that he drank by the firkin

There was a young lady called Wild
Who kept herself quite undefiled
By thinking of Jesus,
Contagious diseases
And the bother of having a child

Now you've a Grown-up's Bath
  Book
You'll not be needing your duck
Just tell him 'So long'
Go back to Hong Kong
As the Americans say 'You suck'

Mrs Mary Whitehouse
Caught sight of a lighthouse
It did not escape her detection
That erection!

Bath-time Sex Games

Moby Dick

This is a role-playing game. The male hunts, the female is the hunted. Generous-sized baths and a female partner of heroic proportions will lend themselves perfectly.

Suggested plot lines are 'there she blows captain' to 'where's my trusty harpoon' and repeatedly thrusting it home.

Our pilot couple actually went to the lengths of taping whale cries, which they played throughout the match, during the frantic highlights someone jumbled the cassette buttons and we picked up cries of 'die, die you great monster' to which came the passionate reply 'if I go, I'm taking you with me!'

True aficionados will of course remember that Queequeg the harpoonist was tattooed from head to foot. We recommend non-permanent red and blue marker pens as they can add more play to the foreplay.

Spin the Bottle

This is an upmarket, top-of-the-range game which requires a substantial amount of floor space. The ideal locations for it are accommodating leisure centres (form your own sex club and hire it) or super luxury personal pools, etc.

Generously apply soapy water to a large floor area. Place four plastic dinner plates on the floor. The female partner places a hand in each dinner plate and a foot in the remaining two.

The male partner now takes a good hold of the hips of his partner and 'spins' her across the floor. He is then free to dart after her and achieve congress.

Added fun can be had by blindfolding the male, with the female shouting encouragement 'left a bit', 'you're getting warm', 'over here you stupid arse', etc. Good hunting!

Foreplay

All the best games are variations on old classics. The preparation for this game is for the female partner to obtain a condom and place it in her mouth. Keeping her hands behind her back at all times she then has to place the condom on the male. You've guessed it: Pin the Tail on the Donkey. Added fun can be introduced by playing the game in the dark, or by one or both partners wearing blindfolds.

At all times no one is allowed to get out of the bath.

'My wife's asking can you cure it... but leave the warts.'

The Mother of all Quizzes
Tick the answer which applies to you

1 When you are in bed at night and she whispers 'I love you' do you:
A. Whisper back 'I love you too'.
B. Feel a burst of affection and slacken your strangle hold.
C. Look around to see who she is talking to.

2 When you are reaching your sexual climax, do you:
A. Make loud moaning noises.
B. Nibble her neck and give her a love bite.
C. Give your hand a rest.

3 You have made love to your wife, do you:
A. Hold her in your arms until she falls asleep.

B. Wipe your willy on her nightie and turn over.

C. Tell her to go and sleep with the kids.

4 If you break wind in the night, do you:

A. Try to cough at the same time and hope she is asleep.

B. Hold her head under the duvet, laughing.

C. Blame her and give her a clip across the ear.

5 If she breaks wind in bed, do you:

A. Take the blame yourself.

B. Be a gentleman and pretend you didn't hear.

C. Light a match to see if you can ignite it.

6 She tells you she is having an unplanned baby, do you:

A. Tell her not to worry, you will manage.

B. Ring the clinic and arrange for a paternity test.

C. Buy a bottle of gin and run her a hot bath.

7 You come home early and find her in bed with the next-door neighbour, do you:

A. Close the door quietly and pretend you haven't seen them.

B. Join in.

C. Nip next door and help yourself to his vintage brandy/young wife, etc.

DO YOU KNOW WHERE THE EXTENSION LEAD IS ?

8 She accuses you of being an M.C.P., do you:

A. Feel horrified... you do your best to be a caring 'modern man', after all.

B. Say she's wrong... you're totally non-political.

C. Thank her for the compliment and let her walk one pace instead of three behind you.

9 You discover your other half unexpectedly in the bath, do you:

A. Say she looks gorgeous when she's wet.
B. Dive in and give her one.
C. Switch on the electric fire and chuck it in the bath.

10 Your wife says she's leaving you for good, do you:
A. Break down in tears and beg her to stay.
B. Freeze your bank accounts.
C. Put up decorations and organise a street party.

Award yourself a score of 1 point for A, 2 points for B, and 3 points for C

How did you score?

Less than 15	If your brains were made of cotton wool, you wouldn't have enough to make a tampon for a canary.
15–25	Make your bloody mind up!
25-30	One of the lads.

Bath-time Habits in the British Isles

Opposite are the bath-time habits of the average British person, who incidentally spends nearly five days a year in the bath, or one year of their lives! We would like to hear from the readers of *The Naughty Bath Book for Grown-ups* on what you get up to.

	England %	Scotland %	Wales %	N.Ireland %
Drink Alcohol	26	31	0	28
Drink Coffee	34	36	0	29
Eat	8	9	0	6
Read	53	60	5	55
Wash Hair	68	68	16	59
Listen to Music	56	53	16	56
Dream	56	68	16	72
Beauty Treatment	70	72	0	62
Talk on Phone	14	16	5	12
Clip Toenails	15	15	11	15
Wash Dog	10	9	0	14
Have Sex	4	4	0	2
Keep Plants	5	7	5	0
Think	1	1	0	1

Taken from the Graham Bath Report – based on 2,500 adults.

Love Is...

Love is... removing your lover's pubic hairs from the plug hole.

Love is... offering to sleep on the wet patch.

Love is... using your partner's knickers for a handkerchief.

Love is... being the one to clean the vibrator.

Love is... making love with the lights on.

Love is... buying your partner a battery recharger.

Love is... two minutes of squelching noises.

Love is... still showing an interest after the climax.

Love is... waking up in the morning and still fancying the person next to you.

Coiffure of Pubic Hair

For all you budding hairdressers – how about trying the following. Look carefully and see if you can spot the difference with our Asian model example – think sideways.

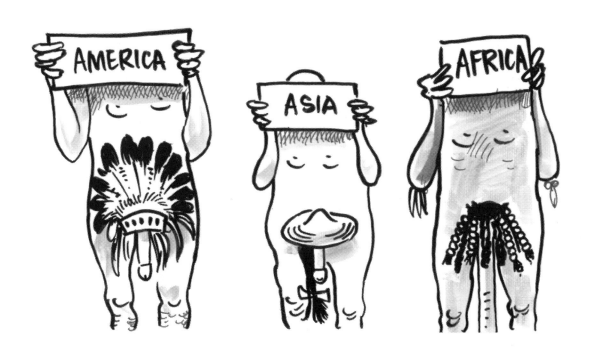

61

Weird Sex

Apparently 200 Britons a year die in similar circumstances to Stephen Milligan – cock or bull?

The answer is true and the Association of British Insurers said that such deaths would probably count as open verdicts which would make them unquantifiable. What would you make of the man who made love to pavements? Or the mysterious caretaker who was arrested in 1992 for performing an undisclosed sex act with a jar of Bovril? The lady who covered herself in peanut butter and let the squirrels clean her up!?

How about a soldier who got his thrills from swallowing Barbie dolls' heads? Or a man who, before therapy, was seriously fixated on his Metro car – 'Its front reminded him of his headmistress and its rear end aroused him.'

NO.. IT'S NOT DROPPING OFF... IT'S A CARBON DEPOSIT.. NORMALLY FOUND ON CAR EXHAUSTS..

Dirty Water Guide

Just compare this page to your bath water and get an instant reading.

You should know better – a bath is for washing in GET F.I.T.T.	Is your partner that ugly?	Make up your mind: wash or frolic!	Excellent but do you have to wash your feet at a time like this?	Would you like to be co-author on our next venture?

Did you know? If you spit into water, the cleaner the water, the further your spit will spread!

How Much Sex can I Have?

Try the following questions on your partner and set your own rules, ie. if he/she gets five right, the winner chooses the position and the loser cleans up the mess afterwards. Think very carefully about the answers.

1 How many animals of each species did Moses take aboard the ark?

2 Divide 30 by ½ and add 10 (no calculators).

3 Some months have 31 days, some have 30 days, how many have 28?

4 You go to bed at eight o'clock in the evening and set the alarm clock to go off at nine in the morning, how many hours' sleep would this allow?

5 If a doctor gave you three tablets and told you to take one every half hour, how long would they last?

6 How many sides has a circle?

7 How far can a dog run into the woods?

8 Which country has a fourth of July, Britain or America?

9 A man built a house of rectangular structure, each side having a southern exposure. A bear came wandering by, what colour was the bear?

10 If you were alone in a deserted house at night and there was a lamp, a fire and a candle and you had only one match which would you light first?

11 How many birthdays does the average man have?

12 Why can't a man living in York be buried west of the Trent?

13 If you have two coins totalling 11 pence and one of the coins is not a 10 pence piece, what are the two coins?

14 How much dirt is there in a 2' x 2' x 4' hole?

15 If two monkeys sit in a corner of a room and look at another pair in another corner and so forth until every pair in a corner looks at another pair, how many monkeys could say that they were looking at other monkeys?

16 Would it be all right for a man to marry his widow's sister?

17 If you drove a bus leaving Croydon with 40 passengers, dropped off seven and picked up two at Addiscombe, stopped at Sanderstead and picked up ten, went on to Purley, dropped eight there and picked up five, then drove on to arrive in London two hours later, what would the driver's name be?

What was That?

Women

Some men try to climb mountains, others try to date them. *Anon*

The tongue of woman is their sword and they take care not to let it rust. *Chinese Proverb*

In various stages of her life, a woman resembles the continents of the world. From 13 to 18, she's like Africa – virgin territory; from 18 to 30, she's like Asia – hot and exotic; from 30 to 45, she's like America – fully explored and free with her resources; from 45 to 55, she's like Europe – exhausted,

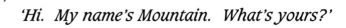

'Hi. My name's Mountain. What's yours?'

but not without places of interest; after 55, she's like Australia – everybody knows it's down there, but nobody much cares. *Al Boliska*

Give a woman a job and she grows balls. *Jack Gerber*

Men

If they can put one man on the moon, why can't they put them all there? *Anon*

Man is the missing link between the ape and the human being. *Anon*

Adam came first, but men always do. *Anon*

The fastest way to a man's heart is through his chest. *Roseanne Barr*

You can take a man out of the bog but you cannot take the bog out of the man. *Anon*

He'd step over ten naked women to get at a pint. *Anon*

The History of Soap

OI LOIKES ME BRISTOLS

In the 16th century, Castile soap was imported from Spain and this is still the name of a white soap manufactured in England and America.

Marseille became famous for soap-making and Venice followed suit.

Bristol was the first English soap-making city of importance, soon to be rivalled by Coventry. Hence the expression 'Lather your Bristols!'.

The London soap boilers produced three grades: the top grade – a speckled variety; the medium quality – white; and the cheapest – grey in colour. Whale oil was used as an ingredient, as was tallow from Russia.

From 1712 a levy of between three pence and one penny a pound put soap beyond the means of the majority in England, hence Thackeray's descriptive phrase 'The great unwashed'.

Soap for the masses came to England with Gladstone's repeal of the soap tax in 1853.

Pears – the long-established firm of soap-makers – began manufacturing their well-known transparent variety in 1789.

Today you can buy soap in a variety of shapes – see Cock and Bull, page 23-6.

The question for readers of *The Naughty Bath Book for Grown-ups* is why are programmes like *Coronation Street*, *EastEnders* etc, called soaps?

A: In America, during the 1950s, it was only soap companies that advertised during the breaks in television programmes that had continuing episodes and these became known as soap operettas. This term was shortened to soaps.

Soap Operetta

Plughole Ghost *by U Rinal*

We recently moved house and inherited a prune-faced gardener. When it was too wet for outdoor work he tended the house plants. A particular favourite of the wife's was the aspidistra which flourished in her great-grandmother's chamber pot. It was kept, naturally enough, in the humid, turgid, bathroom where it seemed to benefit from misdirected jets deflected off the toilet seat.

I digress. There seemed little to do other than spray, dust and polish its leaves. But we suspected the gardener of sniffing snuff and rolling his own for a quick drag on the pan with the fluorescent papered bog roll Aunt Ethel brought as a pressie from Thailand.

It must have been the after-effects of the latter which caused him, uncharacteristically, to pee in the sink to which the previous enthusiastic DIY houseowner had fitted a waste disposal unit. He was dragged into the plughole in a trice by his oversized dibber. Poor old prune-face met a swift, if not painless, end. All we found of him was a mud-stained boot, a truss and a partly digested set of choppers.

The effect on the family has been traumatic. My daughter has been terrified to use the bathroom since the tragedy. The fat mother-in-law is just as jittery. She shivered and shook so much with fear last time she spent a penny it registered nine on the Richter scale ten miles down the road and caused so much stress on the wobbly bits her corsets snapped and a wildfowler shot her down in a farm field the other side of town.

The wife, too, is just as nervous. She takes a bath with her clothes on because she believes the gardener's glass eye, which was never found, winks at her from the slit for the overflow. So convinced is she of this that she has made me put up a sign behind the taps to warn unsuspecting guests 'BEWARE – JACQUES COUSTEAU FILMING'.

Yes Sir/No Sir

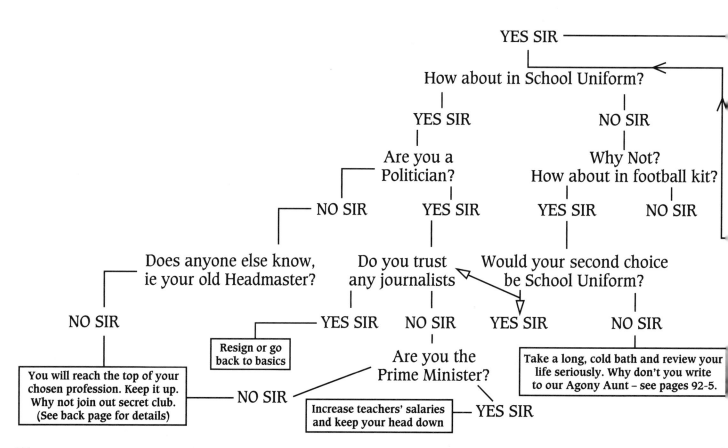

YES SIR

How about in School Uniform?

YES SIR   NO SIR

Are you a   Why Not?
Politician?   How about in football kit?

NO SIR   YES SIR   YES SIR   NO SIR

Does anyone else know,   Do you trust   Would your second choice
ie your old Headmaster?   any journalists   be School Uniform?

NO SIR   YES SIR   NO SIR   YES SIR   NO SIR

Resign or go
back to basics

Are you the
Prime Minister?

You will reach the top of your
chosen profession. Keep it up.
Why not join out secret club.
(See back page for details)

NO SIR

Increase teachers' salaries
and keep your head down

YES SIR

Take a long, cold bath and review your
life seriously. Why don't you write
to our Agony Aunt – see pages 92-5.

After You Bath do You Like to Dress Up?

NO SIR

Do you have any excitement in your life?

YES SIR

Have you ever wanted
to dress up?

YES SIR   NO SIR ⟶

Would you prefer dressing in School
Uniform to making love to a pavement?

YES SIR

Go to box
Are you a Politician?

NO SIR

Then why are you reading this book?
Write 100 lines "I must be more exciting"

NO SIR

Please write to us about your favourite
fantasies – what type of pavement??

Steamed Up

When you get bored of bathing why not visit the local sauna? To give you some inspiration have a look through the following:-

Mensa Sauna

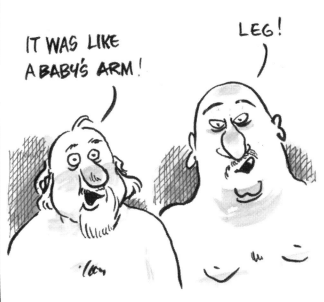

: Steamy Words of Wisdom

STILL.. DURING A STATE OF ERECTION IT DOESN'T NECESSARILY GET ANY BIGGER !

3

BUT IT WON'T GET ANY SMALLER EITHER !

4

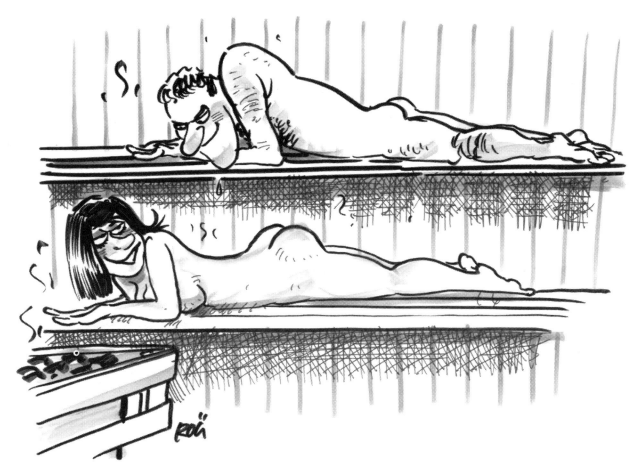

'If you can reach me… you're on!'

'I was fascinated by a bead of sweat... rolling down fragrant slopes and glorious valleys...'

'You've probably heard of the "Mile High" club...
have you heard of the "High 180°" club?'

'DO YOU MIND, MADAM!... This is NOT a tube train!'

79

'I've lost four pounds in sweat and two ounces of semen!'

'AHEM!... Tarzan is swinging between the trees again!'

81

'You mean that bucket's not for if you're caught short?... What's it for then?'

'Ahem... I think you'll find it's a lot easier to raise steam by pouring some water from that bucket on to the coals.'

A Day in the Life of Bartholomew
(Barth for short)

Barth was known for his cleanliness and his total obsession with the word 'bath'. After another wet dream brought on by the thought of being covered from head to foot in bathybius, Barth got up and headed straight for the bathroom to clean up. He tipped the contents of his bubble bath into the bath and had a long soak.

After that he headed off to Bath to buy the much talked-about Bath Books and some Bath bricks. After a fruitless search, and feeling hot and sticky, he made a beeline for the bathhouse to bathe yet again. He put on his bathers and joined the bathing beauties, who were spilling out of their bathing machines and some of the larger ones spilling out of their skimpy bathing suits.

Barth was studying bathymetry and noted the bathometer was giving a reading of 15 feet, almost deep enough to use his bathysphere. The water was lovely, softened no doubt by the bath salts, and Barth now realised how Bath-she-ba must have felt after bathing. Barth had finally soaked long enough and clambered out and donned his bathrobe and sought nourishment in the way of a large sticky Bath bun. Barth is now looking forward to his holiday in Bathurst, Australia, but before he goes he must GET F.I.T.T.

It is all quite bathetic really!

'You're a virgin, aren't you Barth?'

Confessions of a Plumber

Warning!

If you are going to have some private fun in the sanctuary of your bathroom, then for goodness sake, make sure you have a discreet plumber, as you may find yourself in the following predicaments:

'Makes a change from big toes, I suppose!'

'Turning on the tap didn't free you then...'

Virgin on the Ridiculous

How many virgins do you know? I mean over the age of 18 and not in holy orders. For most of us born after the first crusade, virginity is a bore and a curse. Something to be got rid of as soon as possible.

Allegedly, in America, the southern baptists have packed the convention centre in Orlando, Florida, with 103,000 of the gripped-kneed little lovelies. Can you begin to imagine what a room full of 103,000 mixed adolescent virgins is like – the pent-up displaced energy, the dripping hormones, the hysteria.

These aren't just chance virgins, fat girls nobody fancies or spotty louts with over-active grease glands and hydrophobia who haven't managed to get lucky yet. These are professional 'no-go' kids; lithe, hard bodies with perfect teeth and ash-blond hair. They've come from all over the States to sign a Love Waits commitment, a solemn pledge that 'makes a commitment to God, myself, my family, those I date, my future mate and my future children to be sexually pure until I enter a covenant marriage relationship'.

Each proselytising virgin gets a chastity ring (for their finger) that they are supposed to wear until they get married and then hand to their spouse with the words, 'This is part of me for you alone'.

While all the hotel switchboards in Florida are jammed with young men complaining that the water in their showers isn't cold enough, let's consider the future wedding night of the virginal husband and wife. Alone in the honeymoon suite with enough pent-up sexual energy between them to erect a flagpole, and tonight's the night.

'Okay Cindy-Loo, here's my ring. I have saved myself for you, oh boy.'
'Hold on Rusty, we've got a problem. It's stuck.'
'What do you mean, it's stuck?'
'I can't get the ring off, honey. I put it on when I was ten and my finger is too big.'
'Forget the ring, Cindy. Let's just do it.'
'Rusty, wash your mouth out. I made a solemn oath to give this ring to my husband on my wedding night and an oath's an oath. Now if I hold it in the air for ten minutes maybe all the blood will drain out and it'll shrink.'
'I wouldn't count on it, honey. It never has for mine.'

Cut to the next morning. Two maids have come to clean the room. 'Land's

sakes, Beulah, would ya look at the state of this room.'
'Honeymooners, wasn't they?'
'Lordy, just look at all this perverted equipment. Soap, buckets of water, Vaseline, WD40, a file, heavens, a monkey wrench, steak, ice cubes. Don't nobody have normal sex no more?'
'I says the trouble is nobody goes to church no more.'

Agony Pages

Dear Editor,

I am 72 years old and have never slept with a woman in my entire life. I have always had great satisfaction in self abuse. Over the years I have jammed it in doors, squeezed it through gaps, rubbed it with axle grease. Up until I was 60, this was fine but slowly I have been losing sensitivity and have had to resort to coarse sandpaper, wire wool and, most recently, banging it between two bricks or using barbed wire. Now even these practices no longer excite me. Could you, with your wealth of experience, please suggest something to stir my manhood once more?

Ed. Dip it in petrol and put a match to it.

Dear Editor,

My husband and I have always enjoyed a warm, compassionate sex life and, in the interests of variety, have lately experimented with having sex in the bath. My husband, a normally placid and quietly affectionate man, becomes extremely agitated during these sessions. He resorts to foul language which I have never heard before... he abuses me and has even been violent, causing bruises on my body. I am trying to come to terms with this, which only happens with bath-time sex. While I enjoy the vigorousness, I would appreciate any advice you have to stem his profanity and thrashing about.

Ed. Put less water in the bath or let him be on top... he obviously cannot swim.

Dear Editor,

During recent intercourse in the bath my husband let slip my mother's name in a moment of extreme passion. When pressed, he broke down and confessed that they have been having an affair for the last three years. My mother quite openly admitted this and further expanded the confession to implicate several of my neighbours in 'sex romps' while I was shopping. Apparently the whole street has been a hot-bed of sexual activity... she seems to get great pleasure in telling me all the lurid facts in explicit detail. I broke down and told the milkman who became highly agitated as apparently his sister is a lesbian and belongs to the same netball team as my mother. The whole thing is just expanding rapidly and horribly. I don't know what to do next.

Ed. I have sent you the address of a scriptwriter. This could be the break you have been waiting for. Write all the details down and wait for the cheques to come rolling in.

Dear Editor Chappie,

Since my wife and I separated, one has found it extremely difficult to get satisfactory sexual relief. The newspaper media then discovered the existence of one's bit on the side, and now that hubby has found out... no more good time there. The whole scandal has even affected one's chance of a high career post one thought was practically in the bag. What with the lack of sex, I am at my wits' end... what can one do?

Ed. Stop buggering the court jester... you'll only make things worse.

Dear Ed,

My husband is very highly sexed. I'm not complaining, but we have sex five times a night, every morning, sometimes lunchtimes and once each evening. He seems to have a permanent erection. I am so worried that I am failing to satisfy him. What can I do?

Ed. Your devotion to your husband is commendable, but I think that his demands are outrageous and beyond the wifely duty expected of you... you really must cut it out Mrs Bobbit.

Dear Aunty,

I am 35 years old and ever since my mother tried to drown me as a baby, I have become totally obsessed with cleanliness and the sheer thought of having sex with anything, let alone a woman, terrifies me. When I eventually do go to sleep I always wake up very sticky around my lower region and all I can remember is dreaming about baths. Please help me.

Aunt. There is only one answer, Bartholomew, and you will need a lot of puff. However, it should provide endless enjoyment if you look after it. Make sure you go for the deluxe model with real hair.

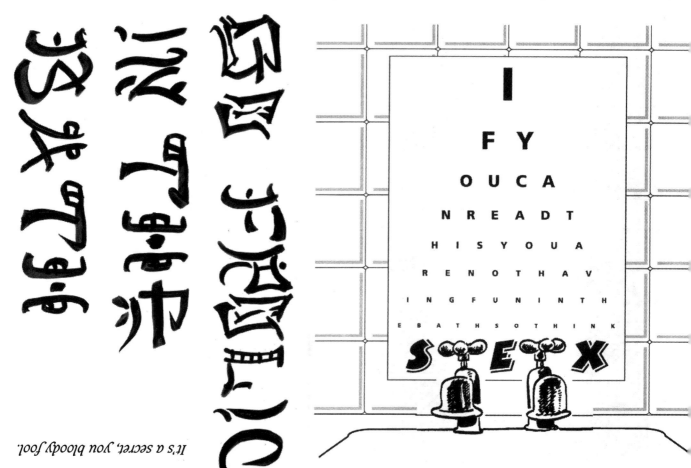

It's a secret, you bloody fool.